BIRDS

by
David Christie

HAMLYN
London · New York · Sydney · Toronto

CONTENTS

Published 1972 by
The Hamlyn Publishing Group Limited
London · New York · Sydney · Toronto
Hamlyn House, Feltham, Middlesex, England
© Copyright The Hamlyn Publishing Group Limited 1972
ISBN 0 600 34811 3
Printed by Mateu Cromo, Spain

INTRODUCTION

Of all animals, birds are probably the most familiar. This is for the simple reason that we see more of them than of practically any other creature. There are thousands of different kinds of birds, found all over the world. And, since birds can fly, they can get to all kinds of places. We can watch them in crowded towns and cities, in parks and gardens, or in the wild open spaces of the plains, mountains, heaths, marshes and coasts. Birds, in fact, are the only animals which have completely mastered flight—bats can fly, but only primitively—and this is one of the most important characteristics that distinguishes them from other animals.

Birds are also familiar because of their beautiful and varied singing. Waking to the chirping of birds or hearing their calls at sunset are experiences which we often take for granted. But imagine how dull and empty our world would sound without bird songs.

Birds become quite tame and friendly with human beings. We only have to take a walk in the park on a Sunday afternoon to see this. Some birds will come right up to our houses and nest in our gardens. In winter, when their normal diet is hidden under the snow or they are too weak to find their own food, even shy birds may come and eat from feeders near houses. In our gardens, we can watch the more common birds at ease; we quickly learn to recognise them, observe how they behave, get to know their different calls and songs, and before we know it we have become amateur birdwatchers.

On holiday in the country or by the sea, we can find still more birds, different ones, and start to identify these as well. We soon learn that the behaviour of these enormously varied creatures can be absolutely fascinating.

In the following pages we will look at some of the 8,600 different species of birds in the world, and learn just how interesting and unusual they can be. The variety of these birds is astonishing. Some are tiny, others bigger than people. Some are drab and others, like the tropical birds, are all the colours of the rainbow. Some spend almost the whole of their lives far out at sea, others lie hidden in dense reed beds, and still others are quite happy in bustling villages and towns. There are vicious birds that attack and kill animals to provide themselves with food, while other birds are tame enough to keep as pets, and if properly cared for, will flourish in captivity.

WATER BIRDS

Many birds spend a good deal of time on, or even under, the water. Some of these have special adaptations for aquatic life. Ducks and gulls have specially webbed feet to help them swim, very much like the artificial flippers used by people. Grebes and phalaropes swim with the aid of lobes, or flaps of skin, along the sides of their feet. The very long toes of gallinules allow them to walk on the tops of water lilies and other pond vegetation.

Water birds, like most birds, have oil glands, and in some species such as pelicans these are specially developed. The oil from these glands, applied to feathers, keeps them in condition and waterproofs them.

Many of these birds are not particularly strong fliers, since life in the water keeps them protected from most predators. Instead, some are expert divers and can swim underwater with great speed and agility, often remaining submerged for a long time. When they are forced to come on to land, they may find walking a little difficult, like the divers when they come ashore in spring to build their nests.

Left: the Pagoda Thrush. This is one of the most colourful of the 306 species of thrush found throughout the world. Thrushes are generally recognised as being great songbirds. *Below:* of the four species of divers, the Red-Throated Diver is the best known and also the smallest. Divers breed in the far north of the world but move further south in the winter.

Birds can live on all kinds of water. Eiderducks and Harlequin Ducks are quite at home riding the rough surf of the open sea in the middle of a storm, whereas some ducks and gallinules much prefer the calmer ponds and lakes of inland districts.

Gulls may be found almost anywhere, from the Arctic to the Antarctic, though they rarely go out of sight of land. Many have become first-class scavengers, and are a great help keeping our beaches and harbours clean. They often raid trawlers as the boats unload at the docks.

Closely related to the gulls, and similar in many ways, are the terns, which are found both out to sea and inland. Most are white with a dark cap and a forked tail like a swallow, which has given them the name 'sea swallows'. They usually catch their food, fish and small sea creatures for the most part, by diving head first into the water. The Arctic Tern probably has the longest migration path of any bird. It nests in the Arctic in spring, travels all the way south to the Antarctic in autumn, and then returns to the Far North the following year.

Cormorants are found throughout the world. Most widespread is the Common or Great Cormorant, which breeds on all the continents except South America. Cormorants are expert fishermen, and have been trained to work for people in Japan! First, a ring is placed round their necks so that they cannot swallow fish; after they have dived underwater and caught a fish, they swim back to a boat, where a fisherman retrieves it, before sending the cormorant back for more. Once in a while, as a reward, the bird is allowed to swallow a fish. Slow-swimming fish and small eels are among Cormorants' favourite food.

The Black-headed Gull is found in Europe and Asia, and usually nests in wet sites or reeds. An unusual characteristic of its plumage is its head, which is dark brown in spring and summer, but changes to mostly white in winter.

This picture shows a kingfisher in flight, probably preparing to dive down and catch a fish in a stream. There are many different types of kingfisher, of which the best known are the Common Kingfisher of Europe, and the Belted Kingfisher of North America.

Many water birds have curious ways of catching and storing fish. The herons, which frequent marshes, lakes and rivers, are such adept fishers that one quick dart of their bill spells the end for a fish or frog. Dippers, who live high in the hills beside swift-flowing streams, can actually walk along the water's bottom, completely submerged, gathering food. Pelicans merely scoop up fish, using the enormous pouch under their bills as a net. Some pelicans hunt in groups, chasing fish into shallow water and then easily dipping in and catching them. They hold the fish in their pouches, drain away the water and swallow them.

At the ocean shores, there are hundreds of wading birds which spend their lives running up and down the tide-line searching for crustaceans. Sometimes these birds form huge flocks numbering up to many thousands. In flight they are a fine spectacle, first showing the dark upper surfaces of their wings, then the pale undersides. Somehow they all manage to turn and change direction together, flashing dark, light, dark, light, all in one closely packed flock.

Probably the two best known shore birds are the Willet, in North America, and the Curlew in Europe. Besides these there are many others, far too numerous to list. One of the most interesting is the Turnstone, with its tortoise-shell plumage, which gets its name from its habit of turning over stones to get at the tiny animals underneath. Sometimes two or three birds will work together to turn over a large stone. The Bar-tailed Godwit is beautiful in summer when its entire underside, neck and breast are a bright chestnut colour. Its bill is slightly tilted upwards and very long, like that of many wading birds, to allow it to probe in

the soft mud for food. The Snipe also has a long bill, which it uses to probe the secluded corners of marshes.

In shallow lakes and lagoons we find birds like the stilts, with their extremely long legs which enable them to wade far out into the water. In tropical salt waters the exotic-looking pink flamingoes, balanced on their long, spindly legs, are to be found. The flamingo has longer legs and neck in proportion to its body than any other bird. It has the strange habit of feeding with its head and bill upside-down. It drags its upper bill in the silt, draws in water by suction and filters out everything but the food through a comb-like organ.

Many marsh birds are very shy and rarely come out from the cover of reeds. Rails, for example, spend most of the day under cover and are active only at night, when they hunt for food and utter wild cries from the reed beds. Unhappily, they are rapidly disappearing from many places as the reed beds and marshy places in which they live are being reclaimed for development.

One of the smallest ducks found in marshy areas is the Teal. It inhabits boggy moors, flooded ditches and the margins of lakes, particularly where there are a lot of rushes. Like the Rail, it likes to keep well out of sight and will only fly out of the rushes if it is disturbed. Teals usually build their nests quite away from the water, perhaps even in a wood. Their breeding season is in May, after which they migrate to various countries.

A number of passerine or perching birds such as finches, crows and thrushes are also found in the marshes, although they more frequently inhabit woodland and garden areas.

The most notable characteristic of the Pelican is its huge beak. The big pouch underneath acts as a dip net for catching fish. Various species of Pelicans are found all over the world.

This colourful bird is a
Mandarin Duck, found usually
in Eastern Asia and Japan.
They can be seen on small
fresh-water ponds, lakes and
inland streams, and are often
kept in captivity.

Jacanas are often called lily-
trotters as their long toes
enable them to walk across
vegetation on ponds and
swamps. Pictured here is the
African Jacana.

OCEANIC BIRDS

Oceanic birds lead very different lives from other birds, as they spend most of their time on the wing, far out at sea. They usually come to shore only to nest in huge colonies on the inaccessible cliffs of coasts or remote islands. Sometimes, however, they may be blown inland by strong gales.

Most people will not have the opportunity to see many real oceanic birds, of course, unless by chance they come across one that has been driven ashore in a storm. If, however, they are lucky enough to cross the ocean on a big liner, there will be a wealth of bird life to be discovered.

Probably the best known sea birds are the albatrosses, whose enormous wingspans allow them to glide along on air currents for long periods of time. They can actually travel faster than ships. There are fourteen species, found mainly in southern oceans, of which the best known is the great Wandering Albatross. It has the largest wingspan of all living birds.

Left: the striking black and white plumage of the Oyster-catchers shows up well as they rise up from the water's edge. *Below:* a Kittiwake is seen in flight. This bird nests on cliff ledges, and on windy days it uses its tail and feet as well as its wings to control its approach to its nest.

Much smaller, but related, are the petrels and shearwaters. Petrels are named after St Peter, because they appear to walk on the water. They flit along, their feet pattering on the surface as though it were solid ground. Wilson's Petrel is probably the most numerous bird in the world; it breeds in the Antarctic and ranges over a wide area of oceans, extending well into the northern hemisphere.

Another kind of petrel, the Northern Fulmar, has spread very successfully in the last hundred years. At the end of the last century it was found mainly in Canada and Iceland. Then one colony was started in the Shetland Islands, and today one of its main strongholds is the British Isles. Perhaps the bird's success is due to the fact that it thrives on waste thrown overboard by whaling fleets and other boats.

Shearwaters cannot walk on the water, but they glide so low over the waves that they seem to sheer off the foam. They are found on all the oceans of the world. In Australia and New Zealand, there are several species, called Muttonbirds, which have a peculiarly pleasant flavour when cooked. The birds are actually tinned and sold as 'Tasmanian squab'.

Another master of flight is the frigatebird, which can soar for hours on end without seeming to move its long, narrow, angular

The long legged Flamingo is one of the world's most beautiful and picturesque birds. There are four different species and they are found mainly in South America and Africa.

wings. Frigatebirds inhabit tropical seas for the most part, and are often found near the coast. They nest in large colonies, usually near other nesting birds like boobies.

Tropicbirds, of which there are three species, are found in tropical and subtropical waters, and are easily recognised by the extra long central feathers in their tails. When not breeding they range far out to sea, although they do not usually reach the real centre of the oceans. They can be very aggressive, and will readily fight with each other over nesting sites.

Perhaps the strangest looking of the oceanic birds is the auk, which looks very much like a penguin, but can fly. One species, the Great Auk, is now extinct. It was as big as a large goose, and was hunted by hungry sailors and others for its meat and oil. Puffins, razorbills and guillemots all belong to this family of powerful swimmers and expert divers.

Many birds are not really oceanic, but are often seen far out to sea in winter, after the breeding season has ended. The divers of the Far North, some terns and the phalaropes are examples. The three species of phalaropes really belong to the 'wader' birds, but they can swim as well as they can wade or walk. They swim rather jerkily, often spinning around in small circles to disturb small floating organisms, which they like to eat.

Albatrosses are the best known oceanic birds, although they are usually seen only far out to sea. There are many different species, and our picture shows a Buller's Albatross, which inhabits New Zealand waters.

GROUND BIRDS

Most birds spend some time on the ground, and many feed there, but there are groups of birds which spend almost all their time on foot, skulking among the undergrowth, searching for food, or running across the open plains, even though flying would be much quicker.

On open steppes large birds called bustards are found. Generally they are shy and not easy to locate, for they run away as soon as they suspect the approach of an intruder. Found all over the world except in America and the cold polar continents, they are impressively large, but so well camouflaged that they are practically invisible when motionless.

In Mexico and South America an odd-looking bird may be seen running along roads and in front of cars. This is the Roadrunner, well known from the American cartoon series. Although you would never guess from its appearance, the Roadrunner is in fact related to the cuckoos. It rarely flies, but can move at incredible speeds, thanks to its long legs. It also has a very long tail, which it holds cocked upwards when running. It feeds on small snakes and lizards which it kills by pounding them with its bill.

Left: the Corncrake nests in grassland and fields, in tall vegetation. It breeds in Europe, but is becoming less common as it is often destroyed by farm machinery cutting the grass. *Below:* the Pheasant is an attractive bird and one that is regarded as something of a delicacy for the table.

In South and Central America we also find antbirds. These shy, skulking birds live in thickets and the undergrowth of forests, where they feed on insects. Some of them follow armies of ants, and catch insects which the hordes disturb.

On the other side of the world live ground birds called pittas. The most curious thing about these birds is the way they catch their food. Besides eating insects, they can extract snails from their shells by breaking them open against a stone which is called their 'anvil'. There are twenty-three kinds of pitta, all of which live in tropical scrub, forests and jungles from Africa to the Solomon Islands. They do not walk or run, but manage to move very quickly, hopping along the ground in long strides. They all have characteristic calls, which give away their presence even though they cannot be seen in the undergrowth.

Perhaps the best known of the ground birds are the game birds —pheasants, partridges and quails. The familiar European Partridge is widespread on farmland throughout Europe and Asia. During the winter, partridges go about in family groups called coveys, and often join up with other groups.

Quails are much smaller, and very wary indeed, seldom seen and more often heard. The Common Quail is found in the dense vegetation of fields and farmland across Europe, Asia and Africa.

The Roadrunner lives in the southwestern American deserts and feeds mainly on small snakes and lizards. It rarely flies, but has been known to run at 23 miles per hour!

It is extremely shy, and will only fly when forced to, skimming over the ground for a short distance and then pitching down to cover again. Often it prefers to reach safety when disturbed by running through the grass. The male's call is unique, and is often rendered in English as 'wet-my-lips'.

Pheasants were first introduced into Europe by the Romans. The males are quite colourful, although the females have drab colours for camouflage. There are more than 50 species of pheasant of which the most widespread and best known is the Ringneck. Some of the more exotic species, such as the Golden Pheasant, the Silver Pheasant and the graceful Lady Amherst Pheasant are often found in zoos. They are breathtakingly beautiful birds, whose natural home is south-east Asia.

The Corncrake belongs to the rail family, and like its relatives it is very secretive and furtive. During the winter it lives in Africa, but in early spring it travels north to breed in Europe, hidden on farmland and in grassy meadows. Its Latin name is *Crex crex*, an imitation of its call, which is usually the only way of knowing it is present. The Corncrake has suffered greatly, particularly in Britain, because of modern methods of mowing grass. When combines go over an area of ground, the nests of Corncrakes are totally destroyed.

This picture shows a hen Pheasant in the snow. Her plumage seems rather dull when compared with the striking colours of the cock pheasant. The hen lays her eggs in early April in a carelessly constructed nest which is often not hidden from sight.

FOREST AND WOODLAND

Forests and woods are the home of many different birds. The most colourful are probably birds from tropical lands. Parrots are familiar to most of us but are seen at their best in the jungles, when their natural colours are very vivid. Perhaps the most interesting is the Eclectus Parrot found from Indonesia to Queensland. The male is bright green and the female bright red and blue. The thirty-seven species of toucans of South America have huge bills, usually brightly coloured. The Keelbilled Toucan's bill is variable in colour and all the colours of the rainbow except violet have been found in it.

The 'kings of the forest' are the huge forest eagles. In South America, the Harpy Eagle dominates the Amazonion jungle. It is the most powerful of eagles and can lift heavy prey, such as monkeys and macaws, vertically off the ground. The Philippine or Monkey-eating Eagle is a rare but magnificently powerful creature which also feeds on monkeys.

Perhaps the most familiar of woodland birds are the woodpeckers. Their rat-a-tat can often be heard in forested areas, as they drill holes in trees in order to get at grubs and insects, which they catch on the tips of their long, sticky tongues. There are

Left: the Yellow-bellied Sapsucker is seen here drilling holes in the bark of a tree in order to drink the sap. Sapsuckers are a species of Woodpecker found in North America. *Below:* a Great-horned Owl comes into land. This is one of the largest of the 133 species of owls which occur throughout the world.

many different kinds, one of the largest being the Black Wood-pecker of Europe, a striking bird with a red crown. The Ivory-billed Woodpecker of America is another large species, which is now extremely rare and was once even thought to be extinct.

A good example of camouflage in a woodland bird is the Wood-cock, one species of which is found in America and the other in Europe and Asia. During the day, it stays on the ground, where its brown and buff mottled and streaked plumage merges into the background, making it very hard to find. It feeds mainly at night, probing the ground with its very long bill. The Woodcock needn't worry about being pounced on from behind while it is

The Wood Pigeon is one of the birds most commonly seen in the British countryside and towns.

feeding, because it literally has eyes in the back of its head.

A well known Australian forest bird is the Kookaburra—often called Laughing Jackass because of its loud, mocking call. The Kookaburra is really a kingfisher, but it does not catch fish and often lives many, many miles from water, in open forest, where it catches snakes and lizards. Unhappily, it also occasionally raids farmyards and carries off ducklings and baby chicks. As Kookaburras tend to raise their penetrating cry just before dawn breaks they are often referred to as the 'bushman's clock' in the outback areas of Australia. Those hearing the weird cry for the first time are often alarmed as it sounds strangely human.

Left: the Woodcock's plumage blends in so well with the undergrowth that it is hard to spot it sitting on its nest. The bird is usually found in marshy areas. The Kookaburra (*right*) is one of Australia's best known birds and, in fact, is a type of Kingfisher. It has an unmistakable weird screeching call.

MOOR AND MOUNTAIN

The desolate landscape of moors and mountains may at first seem unlikely to attract birds, but, in fact, there are many which live at high altitudes. Again, it is the eagles which dominate. The Golden Eagle is often referred to as the ruler of the mountains. This is easy to understand when it is seen soaring majestically above the mountain-tops, or gracefully gliding away from its nest or 'eyrie' on a crag.

Small birds can also survive at high altitudes. The Snow Finch, no larger than the familiar House Sparrow, lives high in the Alps above 6,000 feet. The Brown-throated Wren of Arizona, the American Mountain Bluebird, the Olive Warbler of North America and the South American bush-tanagers are all small, lively birds which manage to live quite well in the mountains.

In the Andes Mountains of South America, three kinds of flamingo breed. They were only properly discovered in 1957, when an expedition came across them 14,000 feet up, in the salt-lake regions of Bolivia. The three birds were identified as the

The Golden Eagle is regarded as the most regal of the eagle species. A standard bearing an image of a Golden Eagle was always carried in front of the Roman Legions to signify the power of Rome.

Chilean Flamingo—a race of the Greater Flamingo—the James' Flamingo and the Andean Flamingo, the latter two found only in the Andes. Smaller than other flamingoes, the James' and Andean are the rarest and second rarest flamingoes in the world respectively.

On lower moors birds are more numerous. The most interesting time of year on this kind of landscape is the breeding season in spring and summer, when many birds normally found in completely different habitats, such as coasts and marshes, migrate to moor and high Arctic tundra to nest. Tundra is Arctic vegetation, about an inch in height, consisting of lichens and mosses. In March, April and May, many birds arrive here from the southerly regions where they have spent the winter. Waders like the Turnstone, Curlew, Sanderling and Dunlin migrate from the coasts to the tundra to breed, along with many kinds of geese and ducks.

The birds perhaps most frequently associated with moorland are the grouse. In winter, when the moors are covered with deep snow, some grouse burrow down into it and make a kind of underground chamber in which they stay to keep warm. They do not hibernate, though, in the way that other animals do, for they remain alert. The most commonly seen grouse in Britain is the Red Grouse, which is recognisable by the lovely russet colour of its plumage.

The Spruce Grouse is found mainly in Northern America and Canada. It is extremely tame, and so is very easy to catch. Because of this it is now found only in remote north woods or protected national parks and game reserves.

FLIGHTLESS BIRDS

Some birds do not fly although they have wings. Often they live in remote areas where there are few predators to escape from. Or they may be such adept swimmers or runners that they do not need to fly. In fact, flying could be a disadvantage in areas where a strong wind could carry a bird off to sea.

Probably the most lovable of the flightless birds are the penguins, with their funny waddling gaits. Although they can move only very awkwardly on land, penguins are very good swimmers. They use their wings like paddles to 'fly' under water, and steer with their feet. On ice, they slide on their bellies. Penguins often live in uninhabited regions but they must always be on the look-out for seals, who feed on them. They range in size from the Emperor Penguin of the Antarctic, which is 4 feet high, to the Little Blue Penguin of Australia, only 14 inches tall.

The Ostrich is famous for supposedly hiding its head in the sand, but in fact it doesn't. It escapes from its enemies by crouching, camouflaged on the ground, or by running. It does not need to fly, because it can run as fast as 40 miles an hour. Once

Left: these Rockhopper Penguins are recognisable by the yellow tufts either side of their heads. They live on islands in the Antarctic circle.
Below: Ostriches are the largest living bird and are found mainly in central and South Africa where they usually live in protected national parks.

common in southern Europe, Asia and throughout Africa, it is now only found in the Sahara Desert and some parts of south-eastern Africa.

Closely related to the Ostrich are the rheas of South America, which are also fast runners. One of the strangest aspects of a rhea's life is the way that it lays its eggs. The female lays up to eighty eggs, in various nests and in other places. Many are wasted. The male sits on all the eggs in one nest.

The Australian Emu is almost as large as the Ostrich, and in areas where wheat is grown can cause considerable damage by trampling crops. To protect the corn, Emus were once merciless-ly destroyed, but now high wire fences and other humane methods are being used to keep the birds off. Reserves have been set up for the disappearing Emus, and they seem to thrive in captivity.

In New Zealand, the strange kiwis are found. Kiwis have virtually no muscles for flying and their feathers look more like the hair of badgers. Shy birds, they are essentially nocturnal. Kiwis live on insects and worms, which they sniff out with their strange bills. A kiwi's bill has nostrils at the tip, something found in no other bird. Once the food is located the kiwi digs it out with its sharp claws. The Kiwi has become one of New Zealand's most widely used emblems. Picture reproductions of it appear on coins, postage stamps and many of New Zealand's products.

The flightless Emu, found only in Australia, was mercilessly persecuted until it became quite rare. Now it is protected in special reserves. Like other large flightless birds such as the Ostrich and the Rhea, it escapes danger by running on its powerful legs.

BIRDS OF PREY

The birds of prey are one of the most exciting bird groups. They are found in all sorts of habitats—woods and forests, mountains, open plains, heaths and even deserts—and are marvellous to watch as they soar and glide majestically overhead, surveying the landscape. If they spot any prey, they dive down suddenly.

There are two kinds of birds of prey, those that hunt during the day, or are diurnal, and those that hunt at night, or are nocturnal. The diurnal birds of prey include vultures, eagles, hawks, kites, harriers, falcons and the Osprey and Secretary Bird. The owls are the most common nocturnal hunters.

All birds of prey have strongly hooked bills and powerful talons for capturing and eating their prey. They are very swift in flight and have exceptionally good eyesight. In fact the diurnal birds of prey have the best eyesight of all living creatures. Owls can fly without making a sound, and can turn their heads round in almost a complete circle, both extremely useful assets to a hunter. Their hearing is so good that they can locate prey, even

The Osprey is the only bird of prey that is able to submerge under water in order to catch its victim. Its feet are specially designed to allow it to grip slippery fish.

in the dark, just by sitting quietly and listening.

The most widespread owl is the Barn Owl, types of which are found in most parts of the world. It feeds mainly on rodents such as voles, and usually inhabits deserted buildings, like old churches and barns. The eagle owls are the largest owls; they are almost the size of a Golden Eagle, and very powerful. Some owls hunt over open ground, quartering it slowly with their wings held in a shallow 'V'. A typical example is the Short-eared Owl of South America and the northern hemisphere. Harriers, diurnal birds of prey related to the hawks, hunt in the same way.

Some of the most interesting birds of prey are found in Africa. The Secretary Bird of the African plains feeds, among other things, on snakes which it kills by beating them with its wings or dropping them on the ground from a height. It has very long legs and ear-tufts like an old-fashioned secretary's quill pen.

Kites are elegant in flight, on long, narrow wings. The Black Kite, also called the Pariah or Yellow-billed Kite, is one of the commonest birds of prey in the Old World (Europe, Asia, Africa and Australasia). Although it kills its own food, it is also fond of carrion and can be a very useful scavenger.

These young Hawks are waiting for their parents to return with the next meal. Small mammals and birds make up the main diet of hawks of which there are many different species ranged throughout the world.

Right: King Vultures such as these are inhabitants of the Mexican and Argentinian tropical forests. Like other vultures they live on carrion.
Below: the Black-shouldered Kite is found in parts of Europe, Africa and South-East Asia. Here we see it acting out a 'threat-display' in front of a Carpet Python.

Vultures, too, live mainly on carrion. They hunt individually, soaring high in the air and covering a wide area of landscape, on the look-out for food. As soon as one of them finds that there is food below it will immediately lose height. The other birds recognise what this means and all make for the same spot in a long, very fast glide.

The Osprey is a fish-eater found on all continents except South America. It catches fish by plunging feet first into a lake or river and simply grabbing the swimming prey in its talons. Special pads on the soles of its feet help the Osprey to grasp the slippery victim.

Falcons are among the swiftest birds in the world. The most widespread is the Peregrine Falcon, which actually knocks its prey out of the air by flying above it and then suddenly diving headlong at it at great speed. Birds like the goshawks fly at birds

Vultures are the last visitors to feed off dead animals. Their beaks are designed to enable them to tear off strips of flesh and muscle.

and mammals in the tree-tops, and usually ride them to the ground before killing them. They used to be widely used in falconry, and were used in Japan for hunting rabbits and marsh birds.

In the same family as the Goshawk, but smaller are Cooper's Hawk, the Sharp-shinned Hawk and the European Sparrow Hawk.

Unfortunately many birds of prey have become very rare. There are many reasons for their disappearance, a chief one being the increased use of poisonous chemicals like D.D.T. in agriculture. When birds feed on prey which have consumed these chemicals, the poison passes into their bodies and makes them unable to produce fertile eggs. The Bald Eagle, the national emblem of the United States, is rapidly becoming rarer and rarer, and the magnificent Golden Eagle is also suffering great losses.

This Screech Owl jealously guards its recently caught mouse, and stares down suspiciously from its tree perch. Like other owls it hunts for food at night.

RECORD MAKING BIRDS

Just to get an idea of the great variety of birds there are in the world, let us take a brief look at the extremes. The Ostrich is the largest living bird in the world. It may grow up to 8 feet high and 6 feet long and weigh 300 pounds. The Emperor Penguin, at almost 4 feet high, may weigh 90 pounds. But these are both flightless. There are a number of large flying birds, and the heaviest of these are probably the American condors at up to 30 pounds. Two more large American birds are the Trumpeter Swan and the Great White Pelican. They are both 6 feet long and have impressive wingspans of 10 feet. The biggest wingspan is possessed by the Wandering Albatross of the southern oceans, whose narrow wings are $11\frac{1}{2}$ feet from the tip of one to the tip of the other.

At the other extreme, the world's smallest bird is the Bee Hummingbird, an attractive bird from Cuba and the Isle of Pines, which is no longer than $2\frac{1}{2}$ inches. It beats its wings 75

Left: the majestic Australian Black Swan can be very aggressive in the breeding season when it will attack other animals that approach its nest. *Below:* the King Penguin is the second largest of its species. It does not build a nest but incubates its single egg, by holding it on top of its feet and protecting it with its body.

times per second as it hovers in front of a flower, collecting nectar. The food requirements of these small birds are very great, since their active existence requires so much energy. A Bee Hummingbird eats half its own weight in sugar every day.

Many other hummingbirds are also tiny, and kinglets, tits and some warblers are almost as small. These birds can suffer greatly in winter and often die of starvation and cold. If they are insect eaters, they cannot find food once the earth is covered with snow. Certain small species have almost disappeared from the hardest hit regions during cold winters and their recovery is often painfully slow.

There is some disagreement over which is the world's fastest bird. The needle-tailed swifts of the Himalayas and south-east

One of the smallest species of birds in the world, the Allen's Hummingbird, perches on a slender twig, while, *below*, the largest bird in the world, the Ostrich, is seen at its first moment of existence as it emerges from its shell. An Ostrich egg is often more than twice the length of a fully grown Hummingbird.

India have been timed in level flights at a speed of over 200 miles per hour and are probably the fastest at this kind of flight. The Peregrine Falcon, and other birds of prey, easily reach the same speed in a dive. Vultures, when they are gliding towards a carcass from a number of miles away, reach a speed of 100 miles per hour and more.

As a group, the swifts are probably the fastest along with the falcon family. They have streamlined shapes and long, backswept wings—like modern jets, which are also designed for speed. The Bat Falcon is perhaps the fastest of all small birds in a dive, and can catch the largest species of swift if it gets above them. When a falcon has killed its prey, it lets it fall lifeless to the ground, and comes back to feast at its leisure.

The Peregrine Falcon can reach a speed of 200 miles per hour in a dive, thus making it one of the fastest birds in the world.

STRANGE AND UNUSUAL

Within the groups we have been discussing, certain birds lead particularly interesting lives, and deserve special notice.

Some have special co-operative arrangements with other animals. For example, the small African oxpeckers or tick-birds travel in groups on the backs of cattle and Rhinoceroses. They feed on the lice and other insects which are found on the animals' backs. Cattle Egrets often accompany herds of cattle in Africa and feed on small animals disturbed by their feet as they move about. It is not uncommon to see a herd in Africa with tick-birds on their backs and Cattle Egrets at their feet, paying virtually no attention to their odd associates.

Another kind of co-operation between birds and other creatures is found in 'anting'. Birds like the European Jay allow ants to stream over them. The ants squirt formic acid on them, which probably helps kill parasites such as fleas and lice. The Jay has a distinct harsh call.

Left: our picture shows a Jay 'anting'. The birds squats on the ground and allows ants to crawl over it. The ants eject formic acid which is thought to kill parasites living in the Jay's feathers. Cattle Egrets (*below*) are usually found in groups, often following a herd of cattle and eating the small animals and insects disturbed by the herd.

The Skua, of which there are four species, is found on Arctic and Antarctic coasts. It is a strong flying bird and is often mistaken for its close relative—the gull. *Left:* this young Cuckoo begins its life in the nest of some other bird. Cuckoos usually lay their eggs in the nest of small passerines who then hatch and bring up the young.

A number of birds live off other birds in various ways. Skuas chase fishing birds like terns until their victim drops or disgorges the prey which it has just caught. The skua then drops down and picks up the fish for itself. The larger and fiercer frigate-birds chase gannets returning from fishing trips. A number of birds, such as cowbirds of North America and some cuckoos, lay their eggs in the nest of other birds. The bird in whose nest the eggs are laid is called the host and it has to incubate the eggs and rear the brood. The anis of South America often share a single nest with two layers, each layer holding the eggs of one pair of birds.

Shrikes have a macabre method of storing food. They catch insects and small reptiles, which they impale on thorn bushes or barbed wire, thus keeping a ready supply of food available. This is called their larder, and because of this habit shrikes are often called 'butcher birds'.

The only bird actually known to have hibernated is the Poor-Will of America, which takes its name from its call. Poor-Wills have been found sometimes spending the winter in caves, in a very deep sleep.

Perhaps most astonishing of all are the swifts. Scientists believe they actually fall asleep in mid-air, while flying. The birds have been seen from high-flying aircraft travelling more slowly than usual and with their eyes closed, as if they were steering by 'automatic pilot'! Swifts, and their close relatives, the Hummingbirds are recognised as the unquestioned kings of flight. As a result they have highly developed wings, but their feet are very small and poorly developed.

These two birds, a Cape Penguin (*left*) and a Spoonbill (*right*) stop for a chat at the Tropical Bird Gardens in Somerset, England.

Left: this colourful bird is the Southern Carmine Bee-Eater, one of the 24 species of Bee-Eaters found throughout the temperate lands of the Western Hemisphere. They eat all kinds of insects which they catch on the wing. However, as their name implies more than half the insects they choose are from the bee and wasp family.

Right: the Crossbill is found in conifer and spruce woods in the Northern Hemisphere, where presence may be detected by the opened pine cones on the ground. Using its unique beak it extracts seeds from larch and pine cones. Our picture shows the male on the right with his brick coloured plumage, and the duller green and olive yellow female on the left.

NESTING

Birds have countless different kinds of nests and nest sites. They nest on the ground, in trees and bushes, in natural holes, in specially excavated holes, on cliff-ledges, in reed-beds, in fact almost anywhere. They may nest singly, in small groups or in huge colonies numbering many thousands.

Some nests are most peculiar. Social Weavers build huge communal nests, a sort of birds' block of flats. Hundreds of birds work together to build the structure. The Tailor Bird gets its name from the way in which it sews leaves together with fibres to form a cup, in which it then builds its nest.

Many birds nest in holes, but the Hoopoe of Africa and Europe never cleans out its nest-hole, so that the nest starts to smell very strongly and eventually is just a stinking mess. Hornbills also nest in holes. The male hornbill seals in the female, leaving just a very small hole through which he can feed her. She stays inside the hole until the time comes for the young to leave the nest.

Small birds living in South-east Asia build their nests entirely of saliva. These are the cave swiftlets or edible nest swiftlets, and

Left: a Gannet and her young in their precariously balanced nest. Gannets breed on cliffs and often build their nests on seaward facing precipices where they can occupy all the space available. *Below:* a Red-throated Diver is seen turning her eggs.

from their nests the Chinese people make birdsnest soup.

Some birds, like grebes, build floating nests on water. Grebes' nests are anchored to reeds or aquatic vegetation to prevent them from floating away. When the grebe leaves the nest, it covers the eggs with plants to hide them from crows, foxes, weasels and other predators. The eggs, white when laid, soon become stained by the plants.

Perhaps the most unusual of all nests are built by the Australian megapodes. First they build a tall mound of earth, and the female lays her eggs in a chamber in the centre. The chamber is then covered over with vegetation, which is left to rot. The eggs are incubated by heat from the sun and the heat generated by the rotting plants. The temperature must be kept at a constant level (92° F) and this is done by the male. He is able to judge the temperature by tasting the earth. Every few minutes throughout the day, he picks up a sample of earth in his bill and presses it against his tongue, which is sensitive to heat. If the temperature drops, more earth is added to the mound. If it rises, earth is removed.

Some small birds protect themselves by nesting near larger, more fierce birds. In America small, defenceless birds often nest near Red-tailed Hawks, and tyrant fly-catchers prefer to nest in the vicinity of Kiskadees, which are so fearless that predators

Left: the nest of this Purple Backed Wren is a typical example of the bulky nests built by wrens. Usually dome-shaped, the entrance is at the side. *Below:* a Jay perches protectively over its young. Jays build fairly large nests which they often line with grass.

tend to avoid them. Other birds are even more remarkable: Some nest beside colonies of hornets, and others even build their nests inside wasps' nests and, incredibly, may feed on the wasp grubs. Nobody knows why these insects allow this.

Birds which nest in colonies, such as terns and gulls, are to some extent protected by force of numbers. Terns usually nest in very large colonies on coastal marshes, shingle banks or sand-dunes. If a person or animal enters the colony or even approaches to within a hundred yards, the colony will rise up in the air and dive straight at its head, sometimes drawing blood with their long, pointed bills.

Sometimes the male, sometimes the female and sometimes both build nests. Usually, both sexes share the work of incubating, although in some birds, like the Ostrich, only the males brood and in others, like chickens, only the female sits on the eggs.

Most birds line their nests in some way or another. The Blackbird for example, builds its nest of moss, paper, dead grass, straw and leaves, and then lines it with mud before placing a final lining of dry grass on the inside. The Song Thrush makes its nest from similar material, but then lines it with a unique 'plaster' which it makes from rotten wood, dung and saliva packed tightly together.

Left: using plant fibres, the Tailorbird sews the edges of one or two leaves together to form its nest. It lines the nest with grasses, animal hair and plant down. *Right:* the White Stork usually builds its nest on the roofs of houses. This has come to be regarded as a sign of good luck, and many people try to encourage them by putting platforms and baskets on their roofs.

DISPLAYS

'Displays' are rituals which birds use to communicate with each other. They are a means of conveying all sorts of things.

The best known purpose of display is to win and keep a mate. Much research has been done on this, notably on the Great Crested Grebe. The birds face each other on the water, rear up with necks stretched and rapidly shake their heads from side to side. One or both birds will dive and bring up a piece of weed. This may then be presented to the partner. This display is frequently seen on lakes in spring.

The Albatross is also renowned for its courtship displays, which it performs throughout the breeding season. Its antics involve various awkward dances, which it accompanies with a lot of bowing and scraping. It also snaps its beak and makes a strange grunting noise. These rituals may be performed by just two birds, but sometimes many birds join in.

Many other birds have evolved displays which are just as elaborate. Take, for example, the mutual fencing displays of the

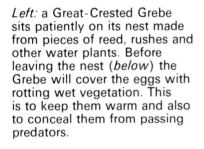

Left: a Great-Crested Grebe sits patiently on its nest made from pieces of reed, rushes and other water plants. Before leaving the nest (*below*) the Grebe will cover the eggs with rotting wet vegetation. This is to keep them warm and also to conceal them from passing predators.

Northern Gannet, in which a pair of birds face each other and fence with their bills. This is not an aggressive display but in fact reduces any aggressive feelings between the two. They are telling each other of their fidelity. Gannets communicate in many other ways. When one is about to take off, it points its bill towards the sky, to tell its mate that it is about to leave and prevent the mate from flying off and leaving the nest unguarded. When the male has claimed his territory and is waiting for a mate, his urge to guard his area is so strong that even a female is not safe if she enters it. Therefore, she hides her bill—the birds' main weapon —from the male to show that she is friendly when she approaches. This is called facing away. Many birds use all or some of these displays.

Some of the most picturesque displays are the dances performed by cranes, peacocks, pheasants, grouse and Ruffs. Cranes perform dances in spring. The male approaches the female and bows towards her. He then starts to leap into the air, flapping his wings wildly. The female becomes excited and joins in, and the two dance crazily about, splashing in the water and on the meadowland around. The male Argus Pheasant dances by raising his very long tail and bringing his long wings right forward over his head. All the time he faces the hen, who more often

A Gannet preparing to land on a cliff ledge. Before it leaves its nest, the Gannet points its beak upwards in order to inform its mate that it is about to leave the nest unguarded.

than not seems to take no interest whatever.

Some birds have aerial displays, notably birds of prey and hummingbirds. The hawk eagles of Africa fly high in the air, suddenly plunge downward towards the ground, then up again, continuing this up and down flight across the sky. The male Broad-tailed Hummingbird dives up and down around the female, who sits in the top of a tree as he performs. The Woodcock displays at dusk. The male flies about 100 feet above the ground with rapid, interrupted wing-beats, uttering a two-note call.

Communal displays are indulged in by some birds. Ruffs gather together in the spring on meadows and each male claims a mound, where he fights with others to impress the females. Females may choose several males and mate with each one.

The bowerbirds are remarkable, because instead of displaying with their own bodies they build bowers for the females. The Crestless Gardener builds a large structure like a tent, with a garden around it. He tends the garden carefully and decorates it with petals, leaves and anything else he can find. The birds of paradise are the most colourful in display and have so many ornaments to their plumage that they look almost too beautiful to be real. There are many other displays used by various species for different purposes and not all are yet fully understood.

The friendly Robin, a familiar figure of the British countryside demonstrates a different side to its nature as it jealously guards its own territory. Both male and female will defend their own plot of land in winter, driving away all intruding birds.

SONGS AND CALLS

The prime function of songs and calls, like that of displays, is to communicate. This involves many things: attracting a mate, warning off other birds, challenging rivals, and of course communicating with a mate or with young. Only males have actual 'songs', long and complicated series of many notes, and these are usually confined to the early part of the breeding season. Both sexes and the young, however, have 'call notes'. These are usually short, and fairly monotonous. Every species has its own special song, different from every other species, although some sound very similar to the human ear. Call notes are often impossible to tell apart.

Some birds look so alike that they can only be identified by their voice. The Willow Warbler and Chiffchaff look almost exactly the same but their songs are so completely different that they are easily told apart as soon as they start to sing.

Some birds are capable of duetting, with male and female singing different notes, one bird starting the song and the other replying to it. This performance often sounds like one bird singing alone. Duetting is found in birds which live in thick vegetation, mainly in the tropics, so it may well serve as a means of communicating with a mate when the two birds cannot see each

Left: a European Robin fluffs out its feathers to protect it from the cold. Its varied and musical song is easily recognisable. *Below:* the Skylark will let out an unmistakable shrill song as it flies up towards the sky.

other. In Australia the Magpie Lark is the best exponent of this art but the African bou-bou shrikes are the most famous of all. Either male or female may start the song and both can sing the whole song. Different pairs of bou-bou shrikes seem to have their own special song patterns, perhaps to recognise each other from other pairs in the vicinity, who may answer but not with the right notes.

Some birds have very conspicuous songs and others have weak or short ones. This is because it is important for birds to be adequately protected. Birds that feed in the tree-tops and birds that are highly camouflaged can afford to sing loudly and for long periods of time as they are either difficult to see or difficult to catch. On the other hand, birds living on open heaths must be more discreet and sing more softly.

Most species have much the same song wherever they happen to live, but a small number of birds have developed local dialects, as human beings have. The best-known is the Chaffinch of Europe, which seems to have a different song in each country and even in each division of each country. Its song, however, is sometimes mistaken with another type of finch, the Brambling, which comes from Scandinavia, but spends its winters in the slightly warmer climate of Britain.

Pictured below is a fledgling Chaffinch. The song of the adult bird appears to vary from place to place.

BIRDS
AS PETS

Birds are very popular pets and are perhaps the most widely kept of all animals. Such birds as Budgerigars, Canaries and parrots are, of course, very familiar cage birds, but there are many other birds which adapt very easily to captivity.

Mynah birds are often kept as pets. They are probably the best talkers of all birds, but can be very noisy and dirty. The Indian Hill Mynah is the most popular and the most intelligent. It will also talk willingly in front of people, even strangers, a thing which parrots resist.

Most birds can be kept out of doors in an aviary, including Budgerigars. Various kinds of finches are quite easy to keep and breed but it is important to know the proper way to look after each particular bird and to make sure that the right kind of food is provided. Zebra Finches and Bengalese Finches are far and away the most popular of the smaller birds and have been kept

The Cardinal or 'red bird' inhabits the warm parts of Eastern North America down to Mexico and British Honduras.

in captivity for years, suffering no ill effects.

In large outdoor aviaries pheasants make colourful pets. Many of the forty-eight species can be kept but it is not advisable to keep the less well known ones as they require special conditions and care and are difficult to keep alive, especially in colder climates. However, the Golden Pheasant and Lady Amherst's Pheasant have long been established as aviary birds and add a beautiful touch of colour to a garden.

Many different kinds of birds can be kept together. Zebra Finches can be kept with almost any other small birds. However, not any combination of birds always works as some will fight others. One of the best and easiest to keep of the small birds is the Green Cardinal, which comes from South America. It is easy to breed but is best kept away from other birds at the breeding time as it is then quite aggressive.

Larger birds such as hawks and falcons have been kept as pets and for falconry but they require a lot of time from their owners and should not be recommended unless one is prepared to give up all of one's spare time. Owls, however, make excellent pets and often become friends for life. The wood owls, like the African Woodford's Owl and the Tawny Owl of Europe and Asia, are the best.

Wild birds that are found lying on the ground with broken wings or legs, will often become quite tame if they are cared for and nursed back to health.

Before keeping any birds one must find out from an expert exactly what will be involved. Things such as diet, perches and cover are very important. If these are all properly provided for, then a pet bird can make a happy addition to one's life.

Left: the beautiful Golden Pheasant is often kept in captivity by bird lovers. Originating in the Eastern Himalayas it can usually be seen in Zoo aviaries. *Right:* the Australian Zebra Finch is a friendly bird which lends itself to a captive life, as it is very companionable with other birds.

ACKNOWLEDGEMENTS

COLOUR
Ardea—I. and L. Beames 13 (top), Ardea—R. M. Bloomfield 44, Ardea—M. D. England 13 (bottom), Ardea—W. R. Taylor 40, Ardea—J. S. Wightman 41; Camera Press Ltd. 12; Bruce Coleman Ltd.—H. M. Barnfather 45, Bruce Coleman Ltd.—Des and Jen Bartlett 4, Bruce Coleman Ltd.—S. C. Bisserot 33 (top), Bruce Coleman Ltd.—Jane Burton 40, Bruce Coleman Ltd.—Bruce Coleman 8, 33 (bottom), Bruce Coleman Ltd.—Jack Dermid front and back jacket, Bruce Coleman Ltd.—D. Middleton 9, Bruce Coleman Ltd.—R. T. Peterson 16; Karel Feuerstein 37; Popperfoto 36.

BLACK AND WHITE
Ardea—F. Balat 10, Ardea—R. J. C. Blewitt 49, Ardea—Tom Willock 32; Camera Press Ltd.—G. R. Austing 11, 23, 35, Camera Press Ltd.—Mark Boulton 38 (bottom), Camera Press Ltd.—Alfred Gregory 46, Camera Press Ltd.—C. K. Shah 34, Camera Press Ltd.—Len Sirman 51, Camera Press Ltd.—David and Katie Urry 14, 15, back endpapers; Bruce Coleman Ltd.—Des and Jen Bartlett 31, Bruce Coleman Ltd.—Frank Blackburn 53, 55, Bruce Coleman Ltd.—John R. Brownlie 30, Bruce Coleman Ltd.—Jane Burton 58, Bruce Coleman Ltd.—James Hancock 18, Bruce Coleman Ltd.—Eric Hosking 47, Bruce Coleman Ltd.—P. Jackson 50, Bruce Coleman Ltd.—Russ Kinne 38 (top), 42 (top), 59, Bruce Coleman Ltd.—Leonard Lee Rue 19, 20, 22, 24 (bottom), Bruce Coleman Ltd.—R. K. Murton 24 (top), Bruce Coleman Ltd.—Charlie Ott 27, Bruce Coleman Ltd.—W. Puchalski 26, 39, 42 (bottom), Bruce Coleman Ltd.—M. F. Soper 17, 28, 52, 57, Bruce Coleman Ltd.—David and Katie Urry 54; Hamlyn Group Picture Library front endpapers; Jane J. Miller 21, 43, 56; Popperfoto 25, 29; Syndication International 60; Z.F.A. 61.